Kiessand & Cam Co.
Fashion E-book

By: Kiesha Gayles
kieshagayles@yahoo.com
Grandville, Michigan

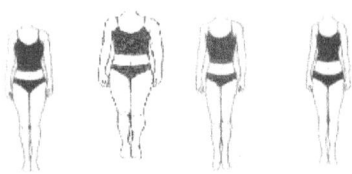

Introduction:

This e-book is design to give Fashion Designers, Sketchers, and other aspiring artists a start to a little direction. Some of us start out without a plan. We do not know the direction life may be pulling us in but there are times when you would like to look around and find some one to help point us in the right direction towards our destiny or the career of our choice. Well for fashion designers, sketch artist, etc. We have put this book together to give you some sort of a direction and information. Grab some coffee and have a seat let us get started.

~Table Of Contents~

****

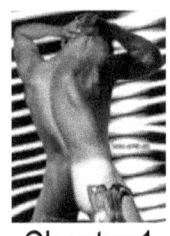

Chapter 1

~ What I would like to do? ~

In the fashion world no matter what you will become, you can always find an outlet to be where your peers are. We look at some designers and think that it is easy to become what they are and see what they have been. We think it is all about putting clothes on a body. Well, in a way designers put clothes on a body, but that body has an opinion they do not like a dress that is too big or colors that do not compliment their figures. We take advantage of some things that we do not truly understand. For example we have fashion sketchers; they have to spend countless hours perfecting a drawing for a fashion designer, or for himself or herself. They have a lot of time invested in there work of creating a design that will fit a certain fabric and/or a body proportion. Then there are the seamstress/ tailor they use a lot of time creating a garment. That takes up a lot of their time. Some garments take weeks, days, even months to create. Everyone in this business has been underestimated in a lot of ways; the value of a good seamstress is irreplaceable. If you never put a shirt together by first thinking a of design and then starting to

drawing a sample on paper. Start wondering what fabric will do it more justice for a great statement. Thinking would it come out the way you seen it in your head. Most Fashion Designers, sketchers nightmare is to see a wonderful design in there head then taking that design to a second party Pattern makers then third Seamstress/Tailor and watching it slowly change from what you pictured in your mind. Some times good talent is hard to find. We will talk more about the talent in our next chapter. We look at the fashion industry and marvel over the Donna Karen, Versace, and LV. We think it is easy to just make some thing and put it out there. No, No, No First you have to look at the facts that those designers worked long hours and very, very hard to get where they are. I am not here to discourage any one, but the fact remains that some designers have it a lot more easier than others do. However, it does not mean you cannot have what they have. Think of what you would like to do. First, start by making a garment if you are an aspiring designer. If you would like to become a sketch artist make a line of clothing. There are also many positions in this business other than a Fashion Designer and a Fashion Sketch Artist.
Those other positions get into a lot of more advanced knowledge.
This book is strictly created for an outline to what you are already thinking. Years of college will handle the rest of your information. But you don't need to go to college if you are a quick learner and have the determination of 26 bulls.

To start off fashion designer should create at least 10 garments from fabric, or drawing. Take it to a patternmaker to create the patterns. Then sit back and relax just for a moment. You want to stay focus and relaxed. Don't over process yourself in the beginning. This career can consume you. Look at the designs and then at that moment figure out who is your market. Try to think of price points for the garment that is in the process of construction. You want to know before the garment is finished what you will sell it for. Then once you figure that out. Think into the future and wonder do you need a partner to join you in your business venture. No matter what profession you may need to take on some one if not for an assistant only. In this business, growing eight arms become possible, and are not very easy to keep up with.

Most business owners do not like to take on a partner. It can have its advantages with a multi task business. If you do not need one, do not get one.

Chapter 2

~Talent~

There are true talents out there. You might want to take the time to find that talent. It will make you grow in ways you could not believe. If you are carrying a talent. It does not hurt to have one extra talented business owner/partner or associate on hand. We live in a world of competition. You get places faster by wowing the competition. If you can build a family through your business partner, associates and agents along the way to the top. You have an advantage. Many business fashion or not always have set backs inside the company due to partner, associates they cannot trust. They spend too much money or do not cooperate with the direction the business is going. You need in the beginning to start a reasonable fashion company. Two designers, 2-sketch artist, 5 sales agents, 3 patternmakers on call. Six-garment manufacturer may seem a little excessive but to have them on stand by is great. As we were stating talent with a manufacturer of being able to keep timely production, creation of the garment is critical. You actually want as many good manufacturers on your side just in case something goes wrong with 3 out of 6 you will have the other three to approach. Make sure all staff can be trusted with your future because it is your name that goes down the toilet if something happens. Hiring family is ok but in any business, you should keep personal and business separate. Take the talented staff that you have rounded up and treat them right because they could be your ticket to success.

Chapter 3

~Money~

How are you going to pay for your staff? Who is going to fund your business? Do you have good credit? I need $ 100,000 for my type of business where do I go.
If you do not have a nice boyfriend or girlfriend. Go to the bank they are sometimes good with interest rates. I do not have good credit. Find a family member with a credit card and convince them as you would a bank that you are a good investment. Well fortunately there are a company called SBA that help many women and minority business owners get there business started. Micro-loans are available. The government does have grant available. You have to do your homework. It is not easy to get to. They do not want to give you something free if they can get you to pay for something as an interest to a loan. You can find the resources. There are a lot of angel investors you may find for the $ 100,000 money that is needed for your potential store/ wholesale project. They are not easy to get to these days either. Unless, you have good connections with some very generous investors. You are in for a serious task to round up the money that is needed for this adventure.

There are programs out there that were built for you to find grants. I looked recently they tried to bury the information. Just wake up one morning with a lot of determination and do a search on Yahoo type in these keywords: grant pro, grant program. Then go to this website: http://www.moneyretriever.com and you will find the most useful information and grant program that were gold for me. Last resort would be to pick up a second job. Carry both projects at once. It will pay off in the end.

Chapter 4

~ Do I Relocate? ~

Most people coming into the fashion world thinking they might have to move to New York, Paris and California to get a good hold on their fashion career. However, that thought is not true. Yes, it would be nice to go to location to be in the middle of the runways and Fashion Capital. You can make your own fashion show wherever you are. You can appeal to the local consumers instead of the total domination theory. Many people do move to New York and do not go any further past their own town. That is because you do not have a plan you should watch your peer. Try not to step out alone because you think you have the backing. Get out there gather information from libraries, stores, boutiques and if do not understand the finer details of the business. Go to a school and sign up for classes. You need to understand Import & Export international and customs if you are not sticking to the USA. Even if you are only thinking of staying within the USA you should try to know about importing and exporting. Learn more about price points, fabric, and manufacturing.

Chapter 5

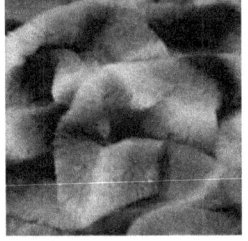

~Wholesaler~

Whether you create a garment or someone else is making the design and selling it at a certain price is very stressful for one reason. You have many things to think about. Whom you are selling to. How much it cost to get the product created. How much did you pay for this product to be created? Do I need to pay for rented space to sell it for a profit? What are the buyers looking for? What manufacturing do I use? Import or Export?

How many can be created/bought. Living in this day an age with inflation as high as ever it is sometimes the biggest thing working against you.

Check out into all those questions above before you think of selling or buying anything. It is great to be prepare for anything.

If you are a fashion designer its feel good to sell your designs to anyone, but if you are selling your designs. Look at the market you are selling to. If you are getting a lot of no's that does not mean your product or garment is bad. It means maybe you are not selling to your market. You may not show this garment or product in the best way. Price points are an issue.

Chapter 6

~Export & Import~

Export to a foreign country means rules and regulations. Got to your state website and look up first if you may need a license. If so, take care of that first.

Become a corp. S-Corp and L.L.C is the best way to go for tax purposes.

Customs are very meticulous on most things that come in and out of this country especially since the last threats. We all know what that mean. On to a brighter subject. Do some reading on customs rules and regulations. Read about how to import and export. Know what ports to use. What type of distribution you will be using. Which is quite important? When your clothes arrive in Los Angeles and you need it to be in Georgia. How is it going to get there and who is going to be responsible for it arriving late. Whom going to check the product before it gets there. Who will take charge of your order? You or someone else? Go to Alibaba there website is GOLD to your business.

Chapter 7

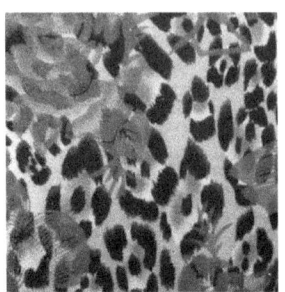
~Fabrics~

Where is your fabric coming from? Overseas or domestic? If overseas, think of the shipping cost. Think about how cheap you can get it overseas but sometimes that shipping price catches up with you. If domestic, they will charge you sometimes an unreasonable price. The shipment is a problem if the order has 50 IBS of fabric to ship. It doubles your cost. Most companies deal with manufacturers overseas because the fee is less crucial. When you are a start up company instead of going to the expensive fabric store, find a good small manufacturer to send you 10 yds. of fabrics at a time. It is less costly this way. Saving money in the beginning is a good way to go.

Fabric store give you a retail price. There are many good fabric manufacturers in California and India. Try Turkey and Malaysia as well. You may need to talk to these manufacturers that are in different countries so try to learn the language. It is far too difficult to get a successful business deal closed if you don't know what you are agreeing to. Some manufacturers give out free samples 30 to 100 swatches.

Very good when it comes to designing a dress and do not know what fabric to deal with.

When it comes to shipping in the beginning process use the Post Office. You will end up winning in the end. Compared to Fed Ex and DHL, USPS you will be charged $50.00 more than you have to. International is the greatest prices set by the post office. Fed Ex accounts are really for manufacturer and big fast growing companies.

~Payments (Bonus) ~

If you are using online orders for shipping international orders. Use World Pay, money orders, C.O.D, T/T for payment for all domestic and International payments. Pay Pal is banking that is more personal. Its get the job done for small businesses as well but it does not accept corporate cards.

Chapter 8

~Manufacturers~

Choosing the company that will create your designs or sell you clothing is very critical to your success. Many manufacturers promise you the world. Some never try to keep the promises. Some even take the extra mile to trap you in an order hassle. You come to the manufacturer and ask them to create the order they agree and they tell you they are taking care of it. However, weeks closer to your order needing completion, you call them up or visit them and find out your clothes is still in a bag. You become very upset. They then start on the product sometimes barely making to the deadline. Some time they do not make it to the deadline. You will have to stay on whomever you may trust with your future and reputation. Many manufacturers know it is not they that take the hardest fall. Always find a manufacture that has insurance. Do not make the mistake of giving your future a snag it does not need. This comment goes especially for new small businesses. Do not hurt your self just because patience is running out and you just want it finished. Do not be afraid to turn down an order. Many businesses take on an impossible task, or a task they know they should not have touched because they need the money. It is better to have a repeated cash flow or a once a while deposit.

If you have a good reputation word, do travel and you will get the big pay off in the end? Keep a good amount of seamstress around just in case you may need an emergency back up for the big and small orders. Make sure you find the seamstress that is not trying to get rich quick. American workers don't want to work for $ 3.00 an hr.

Chapter 9

~Retail Stores~

Retail stores and boutiques are a nice place to start when you are a starter company. Do not try to tackle the department stores in the beginning. We will say it is every one dream to have a good steady order. Money seems to flow if you think of a retail/dept. store. However, think about that first order. 50,000 pcs per color. You have a small company in maybe Mexico that can only supply 16,000 pcs per color. What if the dept store doesn't pay up front? What happens if you cannot pay for the order? What if the manufacturer give you a credit, even if they know you got the Macy's acct. Retail stores that have chains are the same way. Wal-Mart wants you to have certification. K-mart wants you to be financially stable. (We all know why). However, you get there thinking you signing up for that store. Yea right! You might get a store that may supply the distribution. If you are lucky.

Chapter 10

~ Sales Rep~

Hire as many sales reps as you can to cover the region of your target market. Sales reps are gold to a starter business. Please remember not to grow big and throw them away. Because 89% of the reason is where you go with your business will be because of them. I heard many Sales reps complain about how they reach a certain place in the company and they either are fired or are treated badly. That is not fair. You have to remember these people took time out to make you look good. Sales Reps are our good friend. Business is business and common sense is common sense.

There is supposed to be a sales rep for each territory. Think of it as covering the time zones.

Hire nice good people skilled sales reps. some reps can mess up your image if they rep you wrong. Do what they want. You will be shocked what some people can and will do to you when your not looking. Always try to go to your trade shows with your rep unless you trust this person a lot. Make sure your rep is secure with everything they need. Do not send your rep out with practically nothing.

Always make up a package to send them with some starting point.

Sales Reps usual get 5% to 10% of there gross invoice. Some companies will do a lot better for the sales reps. Bonuses are much more rewarding. You will need to have total control over your sales rep for the best results. Watch the presentation at each show. Call every hour if needed. Make your business thrive through determination. Many designers tried to be lazy when it came to having this business giving to them on a silver platter. You should know what you are doing and selling in your business.

Chapter 11

~Website~

At this point, a website should start to be created. These websites can and will cost a lot of money. The cheapest way to get that done is to go to a college and look for students that are seniors that will need the experience. Tell them that they may use your website as a resume. Many are very eager to do so; they need the word of mouth. Fashion sites represent your style. When you do so, do not let them dictate anything to you. You tell them what you

want. They might not know the big extravagant projects or latest designs. Start small work up. Copyright your website. Copyright costs are
$ 30.00 to $58.00. You may print out the form through there website. Look up keywords copyright. Contact your designer for updates which should be free.

Chapter 12

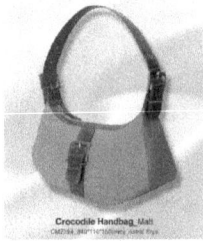

Crocodile Handbag_Mall

~ Advertising/Marketing~

Advertising is very costly no matter what. You can go a cheaper route but to be honest. In this fashion world, we only have certain outlet. Magazines, books, T.V. and Celebrities, website, dept. stores/ boutiques. While we are on the subject of celebrities. They are not a guarantee. Many of us think all I have to do is to get my work on a celebrity and I am set that is not true at all. Some designers that have got there clothes on celebrities did not get any

attention that they thought they would. It is a craps game. The T.V. reporters do not announce the designer and where they are located. Brochures and Alibaba is a must have.
Trade Shows are nice but you don't want to loose money too soon. There is no positive decision that is made by anyone that you will sell something.

Chapter 13

~ Go with The Flow~

Get out there and grab your dream or career. Remember Alibaba for customers. Make brochures for retail stores attention. Use the postal service for your delivery needs. If not use UPS for international. We need to save money.